Research on the EDGE

POLAR REGIONS

LOUISE SPILSBURY

A⁺

Smart Apple Media

Published by Smart Apple Media, an imprint of Black Rabbit Books

P.O. Box 3263, Mankato, Minnesota 56002

www.smartapplemedia.com

Published by arrangement with Wayland Books, London.

Cataloging-in-Publication Data is available from the Library of Congress

ISBN: 978-1-62588-159-5   (library binding)

ISBN: 978-1-62588-575-3   (eBook)

Picture acknowledgments

Cover: Dreamstime: Oriontrail top; Shutterstock: Andrey Pavlov main; Inside: Dreamstime: Antrey 9t, Azaytsev 25, Bernardbreton 6b, Leaf 10b, Mrallen 6t, 28b; FLPA Images: Ingo Arndt/Minden Pictures 20t, Suzi Eszterhas/Minden Pictures 7; National Science Foundation: 18t, Kyle Hoppe 27b, Peter Rejcek 5, 11, 15b, 17, 24, 31, Reed Scherer 22; Shutterstock: 13, Andrey Armyagov 23b, George Burba 19, Deklofenak 26, Steve Estvanik 18b, Paul Fleet 12b, Gentoo Multimedia Limited 9b, Volodymyr Goinyk 1, 10t, Stefan Holm 21, Chaikovskiy Igor 27t, Igor Kovalchuk 4b, Evgeny Kovalev spb 4t, Pegasusa012 20b, Armin Rose 14, 16, Stocker1970 23t, Sergey Tarasenko 8, Visdia 29, Jan Martin Will 28t, Gary Yim 15t; Wikimedia Commons: NASA Goddard Space Flight Center 12t.

Printed in the United States by CG Book Printers

North Mankato, Minnesota

PO 1724

2-2015

CONTENTS

WORKING IN AN ICE WORLD

The polar regions of the Arctic and Antarctic are the coldest, most remote places on Earth. They are dangerous, isolated, and incredibly difficult *environments* for humans to live in. In spite of this, some researchers brave the elements and work at the Poles.

The icy Poles are beautiful, but they are tough and terrifying places to live in.

Polar bears are the largest and strongest land carnivores in the world.

From North to South

The Arctic is a huge, frozen ocean. The North Pole is here. In summer, the edges of the ocean melt, but in winter, the whole area is completely frozen. Antarctica is Earth's fifth-largest continent, covering 5.4 million square miles (14 million km^2). It has the coldest, windiest *climate* on Earth. The land is covered with an ice sheet more than 2 miles (3 km) thick. In winter, the surface of the ocean around the land freezes over. The South Pole is Antarctica.

Working with strangers in a barren, harsh environment far from family and home is challenging, but scientists come here because the Arctic and Antarctic are perfect places for them to carry out their research.

Visiting Scientists

Scientists from all over the world visit the Arctic and Antarctic to study the polar lands. They examine wildlife and how animals survive life in this natural freezer, and look at how *climate change* is affecting these regions. This book looks at how scientists do their research, who pays for it, what researchers do with their results, and some of the discoveries they have made.

DANGER!

Arctic researchers have to be on the lookout for polar bears. Polar bears do not normally attack humans, but a starving bear would catch and kill prey as big as a person in order to feed itself and its hungry cubs. A polar bear can outrun a human and kill a person with one swipe of its powerful paws and massive claws.

CREATURES OF THE ICE

Many researchers at the Poles study its wildlife. They examine the ways in which human activities and climate change affect different creatures.

> Fishing is a problem for gentoo penguins such as these. The birds get caught in nets and the small fish they feed on are caught by fishing boats.

Numbers of Emperor penguins have declined by up to half in some places. Scientists are researching the reasons for this.

Penguins in Peril

Scientists investigate penguin populations to find out how fishing and climate change affect the birds. One of the ways they do this is by implanting tags in the birds. The tags send coded signals to a computer each time a penguin walks past a gateway built between its colony and the sea. The signals tell scientists the tag number and the time and direction of travel. This *data* is then used to work out how often each penguin goes hunting and how long it spends finding food. When penguins spend longer times hunting, scientists know there is less food available.

Tracking Polar Bears

Researchers have different ways of studying polar bears. They may watch the bears using binoculars, look for evidence of their presence (such as partially eaten seals), or follow bear footprints in the snow (usually overhead in aircraft). Scientists may also stun polar bears and then fit them with radio tracking collars. These send signals by *satellite* to a receiving station. There, researchers use a computer program to plot the polar bears' paths. By tracking their movements, scientists learn things such as how the bears follow the ice as it melts in summer, which they rely on for hunting seals.

CUTTING EDGE

The radio tracking collars fitted to polar bears are made from the same material used in the conveyor belts in frozen-food factories. This special plastic sheds water and ice, and stays flexible in cold temperatures. The material is so strong that the bears cannot easily tear off the collars.

Only female polar bears are fitted with radio collars. Male polar bears have necks wider than their heads, so the collars would fall off!

DEEP-FREEZE GEAR

To do their work, researchers need equipment designed to withstand the coldest deep freeze! In polar regions, weather conditions can change rapidly, so researchers doing fieldwork carry emergency equipment with them, even if they intend to only be out for a day. They also have to carry spare batteries wherever they go because batteries do not last long in the freezing temperatures at the Poles.

Out on the Ice

Radios and portable satellite phones are vital pieces of gear. They allow scientists in the field to communicate with research stations. In turn, the stations have satellite links to the outside world. Teams also take tents, sleeping bags, stoves, food and other supplies when they do fieldwork. If they are camping for weeks at a time while conducting studies, they take special pyramid-shaped tents that withstand high winds and wind-blown snow and ice.

Inside field tents, researchers sleep in feather-filled sleeping bags, inflatable airbeds, and sheepskins.

On and in the Water

Some scientists research *pollution* in polar waters, or study the living things found below the water's surface. These scientists need boats and diving equipment. Moving ice and sudden changes in the weather make exploring freezing water very dangerous, so boats are fitted with safety equipment including first-aid kits, flares, and other signaling devices. If diving, researchers wear layered *neoprene* suits, gloves, boots, and hoods. They use special freeze-protected regulators that feed them air from scuba tanks.

It is dangerous to leave the lab when a blizzard whips up outside.

Icebreakers are ships with strengthened hulls that plough through ice to deliver equipment to polar stations.

DANGER!

Equipment used in polar expeditions is in constant danger. Windblown snow buries gear, and cracks in ice may open up and swallow equipment in an instant. Ice can build up on and inside devices causing them to freeze and stop working. On water, winds can suddenly whip up high waves that throw equipment overboard, and *icebergs* can damage floating gear.

SCIENCE ON THE MOVE

Getting around at the Poles can be extremely difficult and dangerous for researchers. Some places are accessible only by foot because the snow is melting fast or because of the risk of accidentally driving into a crevasse. A crevasse is a deep, steep-sided crack in an ice sheet that may not be very wide at the surface, but can be more than 98 feet (30 m) deep!

Inflatable boats are light to transport to the Poles and easy to maneuver in icy waters.

Snowmobiles can travel at about 50 miles per hour (80 km/h) across the snow.

Traveling over Snow

When scientists have to walk on snow, they wear wide snowshoes to stop them from sinking. In areas of solid snow or ice, researchers can ride on all-terrain vehicles or snowmobiles. Snowmobiles are motorized sleds that have rubber tracks with rough treads to stop them from sinking and help them to grip slippery snow. Scientists also use tractors with caterpillar tracks that can tow large sleds carrying equipment. Some vehicles are fitted with a snowplow to clear snow when it piles up.

Flying and Sailing

If scientists have to travel long distances to collect data and conduct studies, they often go in special airplanes that have large, retractable skis. These skis can be lowered so that the planes can land on snow and ice. Other scientists travel out to do fieldwork on rigid, inflatable boats.

CUTTING EDGE

Hagglund trucks are designed for traveling over areas of frozen ocean or sea ice. Their wide rubber tracks grip even the roughest terrain. They can also float if driven over a weak spot in the sea ice. The treads provide propulsion so scientists can actually drive and steer while floating. The trucks also have pumps that help to keep out water, and roof hatches that allow researchers to get in and out of the vehicle while staying dry.

Planes ferry people and supplies to and from polar labs, but poor conditions can often ground aircraft for several days.

SUMMER SCIENCE

In winter, the Poles are in darkness 24 hours a day, and temperatures can drop drastically. In the Arctic, they can go below -67°F (-55°C), while at the South Pole, the lowest temperature recorded is -129°F (-89°C). Although it is still bitterly cold in the summer, it is light all day, so this is when most researchers do their fieldwork.

Working in the Light

Long hours of daylight allow scientists plenty of time to set up equipment in remote spots and visit it to collect information, or to carry out daily tests, for example with *weather balloons*. If scientists set up test equipment in distant spots and have to return to collect data, they must leave it with *GPS* locators or they would never find it again in the vast expanses of empty white space.

Weather balloons carry a small package of instruments into the air. These measure the temperature, pressure, and humidity of the air they pass through and send the data back to stations on the ground.

> GPS locators intercept signals from satellites in space and calculate how far away each satellite is based on how long it took for the messages to arrive. Using this information from several satellites, it can pinpoint locations on land.

Scientists use daylight hours in the Arctic to set up and check on or repair weather stations such as this one.

Working with Local People

People have lived in the Arctic for thousands of years. Researchers at the North Pole often work with local *Inuit* hunters who have expert knowledge of the environment and its wildlife. For example, scientists have learned from local hunters that the narwhal's unicorn-like tusk is not for fighting other narwhals but is a sensory organ, used for detecting changes in the ocean environment.

PROTECTING THE POLES

The Poles are some of the last truly wild places on Earth and home to important habitats and an amazing range of wildlife. These areas are also fragile and easily disturbed, so scientists try to have zero impact on the environment as they work there.

Waste Worries

In the early days of polar research, scientists dumped waste on the ice or in the sea. There are still piles of waste, such as old fuel drums, in some areas. This type of pollution damages wildlife and habitats. Today, all waste is removed or disposed of more carefully. Labs have sewage-treatment plants that clean waste water from toilets and sinks so it can be discharged safely into the sea. Other waste is packed up and removed by ship or burned in an *incinerator*. Any remaining ash is then removed by ship.

This turbine converts the energy from wind into electricity for researchers to use in Antarctica.

Removing waste such as these abandoned oil drums from remote places in Antarctica is so difficult and expensive that the waste is left to litter the landscape.

CUTTING EDGE

At Rothera Antarctic research station (see page 17), fresh water is provided using reverse osmosis filtration technology. In this system, seawater is passed through special membranes (thin materials) that remove salts and other impurities, leaving fresh water. This process uses much less energy than that which is required to melt snow.

Reducing Impacts

Research stations need electricity to power heaters, stoves, laptop computers, and other equipment, but burning oil causes pollution and releases *carbon dioxide* into the atmosphere. To overcome this, research labs install *solar energy* systems, which generate electricity using the abundant sunlight at the Poles. Solar power also reduces the amount of fuel that has to be delivered to the research stations by ship, which further reduces energy use and pollution.

It's vital for scientists to disturb animals such as this leopard seal as little as possible so they can study how they behave naturally in the wild.

POLAR LABS

Scientists carrying out research on the edge need research stations—buildings in which they can live and work. There is a range of these labs at the Poles.

Purpose-Built Labs

Some Arctic research labs are on islands or land skirting the Arctic Ocean, such as the northern parts of Canada. However, to get really close to the North Pole, the labs have to be situated on giant floating blocks of ice. This means that they are constantly moving. In the Antarctic there are large, permanent stations. All polar labs are made from materials brought to the Poles for this purpose because there are no trees there to supply wood for building. People often build bases on legs to keep the floors off the freezing, icy ground and to stop snow from piling up in front of doors and trapping researchers inside.

Antarctic mobile homes like these can be dragged on sledges to new locations.

Some semi-permanent field camps use easy-to-assemble huts like these Jamesway tents, built from *insulated* double-walled canvas stretched over arches of wood.

CUTTING EDGE

Halley VI, a new British Antarctic research station, began operating in 2013. It is the first fully relocatable research station, mounted on *hydraulic* ski-legs that can be raised so that it does not become trapped by snow and can be towed to a new location.

A Typical Research Station

Rothera research station in Antarctica is built at the southern end of an island. There are offices, bedrooms, a dining room, a kitchen, and recreational facilities for researchers. The Bonner Laboratory is a large building with research facilities including a seawater aquarium where Antarctic marine life is studied. There is a runway and a hangar for airplanes and a wharf for ships to dock. There are bulk fuel storage tanks and a garage where vehicles are stored and repaired.

LIFE IN THE LAB

Daily life at the Poles involves a constant battle against the freezing temperatures.

In the Antarctic, for example, icy winds of 200 miles per hour (320 km/h) can flash-freeze bare skin in a matter of seconds.

Layering Up

When venturing outside for fieldwork or moving between buildings at the research station, scientists avoid thick clothes that make them sweat because sweat can freeze on the body. Instead they wear a system of breathable under layers, heavily insulated middle layers, and weatherproof outer layers. In summer, sunlight reflects off the snow and burns skin quickly, so scientists wear sunscreen on their lips, ears, chin, and under their nose.

Scientists working outside in low temperatures always wear a hood, gloves, a hat, and a scarf.

In extreme cold, it is important to pull drawstrings on all clothing tight to cover bare skin and to stop cold air from getting in.

Eating Up

People working at the Poles need to eat at least one and a half times the amount of food than normal. This is because the body uses more than half of its total *calorie* intake trying to keep warm. Ships and airplanes have to deliver food, such as frozen vegetables, steaks, egg solids, and dehydrated foods, to research stations. The air is so dry at the Poles that people need up to 1.8 gallons (8 l) of water a day to survive. They get it mostly by melting ice and snow.

DANGER!

Hypothermia is a common cause of death at the Poles. This is when a person becomes so cold that his or her body processes gradually slow down and eventually stop working. Hypothermia is especially dangerous because it stops someone from thinking clearly. He or she can become seriously ill without realizing it soon enough to take action.

Researchers also wear sunglasses when working outside because sunlight shining off snow can damage eyes so badly that it causes *snow blindness*.

FREEZE UNDER THREAT

Many scientists research the effects of climate change at the Poles and how this could impact the rest of the world. For example, if polar ice sheets melt, there will be a dramatic increase in sea levels all over the world.

Climate Data

Scientists collect data about climate change at the Poles in different ways. Measurements from weather balloons above the Antarctic show that the atmosphere below 5 miles (8 km) has warmed in the past 30 years. Measurements of ocean temperatures reveal that

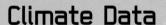

The white, ice-covered Poles reflect the Sun's rays, but this will change as more ice melts.

Some scientists use a magnaprobe. This is a long pole with a GPS locator that measures snow depth and records data when it is pushed into the snow.

in someareas of the Antarctic, temperatures have increased by 0.9°F (0.5°C) per decade. Scientists also use photographs taken by airplanes and satellite images to measure how Arctic sea ice is shrinking.

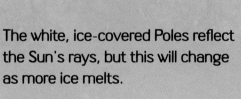

Arctic

Antarctic

Antarctica is the largest mass of ice on the planet. As this ice melts it increases the amount of water in the oceans.

Measuring Ice Mass

Scientists use floating devices called ice mass balance buoys (IMBs) to measure changes in ice thickness over the year. This tells scientists how much new ice builds up each winter and how much ice melts each summer. If more ice is lost than forms each year, there will be a rise in sea level. Using research techniques such as this, scientists can show how melting sea ice also increases *global warming*. When polar ice melts, this exposes dark areas of soil and ocean that absorb the Sun's rays and increase temperatures, melting more ice.

CUTTING EDGE

In 2013, The National Aeronautics and Space Administration (NASA) developed a new solar-powered robot that can take radar images underground at remote polar areas. The images help researchers to study how snow builds up, forming layer upon layer of ice over time on the massive Greenland ice sheet.

CLIMATE CLUES

Scientists have made many important discoveries at the Poles, from the link between greenhouse gases and climate change to other human impacts on Earth's atmosphere.

Changing Climates

In 2004, scientists drilled a 1.9-mile (3-km) ice core, a cylindrical section of ice, from the Antarctic. Each layer of this ice core was made up of snow that fell in the past 800,000 years. Scientists measured the amounts of carbon dioxide and *methane* within bubbles of air trapped inside the ice to learn how much of these *greenhouse gases* were in the atmosphere at that time. The thickness of ice layers and chemicals in each layer told them when Earth had hot or cold climates in the past. By comparing the discoveries, scientists proved that when Earth was warmer, levels of greenhouse gases in the atmosphere were higher. This is how they determined that putting more greenhouse gases into the air causes global warming.

Drilling thousands of feet (meters) in freezing temperatures, extracting ice cores, and transporting them to labs for analysis is a major feat!

Ozone Hole

Since 1956, scientists have been studying and measuring ozone, a colorless gas in the atmosphere. In 1985, they discovered a hole in the ozone layer above Antarctica. By 2000, data from NASA satellites showed that the Antarctic ozone hole had grown to the largest on record, covering 10.5 million square miles (27.2 million km^2). Researchers worked out that ozone was being destroyed by chlorofluorocarbons (CFCs)—the chemicals once used in refrigerators, air-conditioners, and aerosol spray cans.

One way in which people increase the amount of greenhouse gases in the atmosphere is by burning coal and other fossil fuels, for example in power stations.

ozone layer

DANGER!

A hole in the ozone layer is dangerous because ozone absorbs harmful *ultraviolet* rays, preventing most of them from reaching us on the ground. This is important because ultraviolet rays can cause sunburn and lead to skin *cancer*.

The ozone layer is about 9 to 18 miles (15 to 30 km) above Earth's surface.

VITAL RESEARCH

It costs vast amounts of money to build, transport, and maintain labs at the Poles and to pay for research equipment and scientists' salaries. Who pays for this research and who benefits from it?

Funding Research

The Antarctic Treaty is an international agreement that ensures the South Pole can be used only for scientific research that is shared and made freely available. The work there is paid for by different countries' government research programs, such as USAP, the United States Antarctic Program. Some of the same governments pay for research at the Arctic, too. However, the Arctic is not protected in the same way, so oil and gas companies fund research there for their own interests. These companies hope to discover more pockets of oil that can be drilled. They also study the environmental impact of their exploratory oil-drilling plans.

Most scientists who conduct research at Antarctica are funded by government research programs.

There may be rich oil reserves in Antarctica. Will drilling rigs be seen there, too, if funding for research continues?

Bioprospecting

Many privately owned companies want to be able to research both Poles more freely for *bioprospecting*, or finding and using natural resources to make medicines and other products. To make it worth investing in research, companies buy licenses called *patents*, which give them exclusive use of any discoveries they make during their research. If this happens in the Antarctic, it would mean research carried out there would no longer be freely shared. Increased drilling and exploration will also put the environments at the Poles at risk.

CUTTING EDGE

Some types of polar fish survive icy waters because they have a chemical in their bodies that stops them from freezing. Researchers are looking at this substance to see how it could help them improve fish-farm production in cold climates, extend the shelf-life of frozen food, and improve the preservation of transplanted body parts.

SHARING SCIENCE

Scientists working on the edge do research to come up with findings that they can share with other scientists and the rest of the world, to make a difference to people's daily lives.

Acting on Results

When scientists discover something new, they write up their results in scientific journals or present them at conferences. Other scientists read or hear their ideas and decide whether or not they agree. When a group of scientists agrees on a discovery, they pass their findings to newspapers and other *media*, governments, and charities so that the facts can be used to bring about change. For example, the discovery of the hole in the ozone layer over the Poles led to a world ban on CFCs in 1987. It is thought this action could close the ozone hole by 2050.

An important part of research is writing up and sharing research with other scientists.

Several pounds (kilograms) of krill caught by fishing vessels such as this must be fed to salmon in order to produce just 1 pound (0.5 kg) of salmon.

Keeping Krill

Tiny crustaceans called krill are vital to polar food webs. They are eaten by some whales and by fish that are in turn eaten by penguins and other animals. Global warming has caused a drop in krill numbers because krill eat algae that grow on the underside of sea ice, and that ice is melting. People also catch krill to make products such as health supplements and food for farmed fish. Evidence from scientists about falling krill numbers has led to restrictions on the amount of krill that fishermen are allowed to catch.

Without krill, most living things in the Antarctic would disappear!

CUTTING EDGE

Scientists used to have to wait weeks or months to hear about new research. Today, science bloggers and online journals use the Internet to spread, present, or share facts, discoveries, and pictures.

27

SECRETS IN THE SNOW

Scientists have learned many lessons from the Poles, and if these fragile regions are protected, they could discover many more of its secrets in the future.

Researching Impacts

There is much debate today about how much industry and tourism to allow at the Poles. Many scientists are involved in researching the potential impacts of such changes in order to help the international community set limits or controls on them. Some countries are also focusing more efforts on *renewable energy*, such as solar and wind power, to put a brake on climate change. They hope that the polar environments will remain as they are for many years to come.

Many researchers on the edge at the Poles focus their efforts on studying the effects of climate change in the future.

Warmer temperatures at the Poles and melting sea ice are making it easier for oil and mining companies to drive ships farther into these isolated regions, and for tourism companies to bring trips there.

Predicting Climate Change

Arguably, the most important thing scientists have learned from research at the Poles is that if too much ice melts, this could accelerate climate change and increase sea levels, flooding some islands and coastal areas. Therefore, the most pressing areas of research in the future will be to monitor global warming. Keeping the polar regions pristine will allow scientists to continue their research into how the Poles are responding to climate change. Scientists can then provide governments with accurate information so that they can make decisions and choices to preserve polar ice.

Using renewable energy, such as wind power, is one way in which the world can tackle the threat of climate change at the Poles.

CUTTING EDGE

Using new technology scientists have combined 50 years of data and millions of new measurements from satellites and airplane surveys to make a computer model of the ground beneath the Antarctic. This 3-D map, called Bedmap2, will help researchers understand how thick Antarctic ice is and how it will react to a changing climate.

GLOSSARY

bioprospecting The search for plants and animals from which medicines and other products can be designed or made.

calorie A measurement of the energy in food.

cancer A disease caused by an uncontrolled spread of abnormal cells in the body.

carbon dioxide A gas in the atmosphere that is linked to global warming.

climate The usual pattern of weather that happens in a place.

climate change Changes in the world's weather patterns caused by human activity.

data Facts and statistics.

environment The natural world in which plants and animals live.

food web A sequence of plants and animals that are linked together because each one eats or is eaten by another.

fossil fuel Fuel such as coal, oil or gas that is formed from the remains of plants and animals that died millions of years ago.

global warming Changes in the world's weather patterns caused by human activity.

GPS (Global Positioning System) A system that uses signals from satellites in space to locate positions on Earth.

greenhouse gas A gas that traps heat in the atmosphere.

hydraulic A term that refers to a machine operated by applying pressure to liquid in a tube.

iceberg A huge mass of ice formed from fresh water floating in the ocean.

incinerator A device that burns waste at high temperatures.

insulated Covered in something that reduces or prevents the flow of heat, sound, or electricity.

Inuit Native people of the Arctic, once called Eskimos.

media Newspapers, television, the Internet, and other ways in which information is relayed to the public.

methane A colorless, odorless, gas that can contribute to global warming.

neoprene A rubber-like substance used to make wetsuits.

patent A document that gives a person or a company the sole right to use, make, or sell an invention or new product.

pollution When air, soil, or water are spoiled or made dirty or harmful by something else.

renewable energy Energy that can be replaced.

satellite Man-made equipment that orbits Earth.

snow blindness A temporary blindness caused by light reflecting off snow.

solar energy Energy made from sunlight.

ultraviolet Invisible rays in sunlight that can damage skin.

weather balloon A balloon that carries instruments to measure and transmit data about weather features such as air pressure, humidity, and temperature.

FURTHER READING

Books

Earth's Last Frontiers: Arctic Tundra. Ellen Labrecque, Raintree, 2013.

Eyewitness Guides: Arctic and Antarctic. Dorling Kindersley, 2012.

Scientists in the Field: The Polar Bear. Peter Lourie, Houghton Mifflin, 2012.

Travelling Wild: Expedition to the Arctic. Alex Woolf, Gareth Stevens, 2014.

Watery Worlds: Polar Seas. Jinny Johnson, Franklin Watts, 2012.

Websites

See live webcams of United States Antarctic Research Program labs and learn more about the continent and what research its scientists are doing at:
www.usap.gov/usapgov/aboutTheContinent/index.cfm?m=2

This British Antarctic Survey site tells you all about this organization's research at the South Pole and much more at:
www.antarctica.ac.uk/bas__research/science/polar.php

Meet some of the scientists working for the Australian Antarctic Division at:
www.antarctica.gov.au/science/meet-our-scientists

Go on a science mission to study krill at:
news.nationalgeographic.com/news/2013/08/130817-antarctica-krill-whales-ecology-climate-science/

INDEX